RISING STARS
Mathematics

Half-termly
Assessments

Year

1

Steph King
Series Editor: Cherri Moseley

Although every effort has been made to ensure that website addresses are correct at time of going to press, Rising Stars cannot be held responsible for the content of any website mentioned in this book. It is sometimes possible to find a relocated web page by typing in the address of the home page for a website in the URL window of your browser.

Hachette UK's policy is to use papers that are natural, renewable and recyclable products and made from wood grown in sustainable forests. The logging and manufacturing processes are expected to conform to the environmental regulations of the country of origin.

Orders: please contact Bookpoint Ltd, 130 Park Drive, Milton Park, Abingdon, Oxon OX14 4SE. Telephone: (44) 01235 400555. Email: primary@bookpoint.co.uk.

Lines are open from 9 a.m. to 5 p.m., Monday to Saturday, with a 24-hour message answering service. Visit our website at www.risingstars-uk.com for details of the full range of Rising Stars publications.

Online support and queries email: onlinesupport@risingstars-uk.com

ISBN: 978 1 5104 2542 2

© Rising Stars UK Ltd 2017

First published in 2017 by
Rising Stars UK Ltd, part of the Hodder Education Group,
An Hachette UK Company
Carmelite House
50 Victoria Embankment
London EC4Y 0DZ
www.risingstars-uk.com

Impression number   10 9 8 7 6 5 4 3 2 1

Year   2019 2018 2017

Author: Steph King
Series Editor: Cherri Moseley
Publishers: Alexandra Riley and Rachel Menzies
Development Editor: Joan Miller
Editorial: Lynette Woodward, Debbie Allen and Gareth Fernandes
Cover design: Julie Martin
Illustrations by Oxford Designers and Illustrators and Aptara

Typeset by Aptara
Printed by Ashford Colour Press

A catalogue record for this title is available from the British Library.

Contents

Introduction

Why use *Rising Stars Mathematics Half-termly Assessments*?

The *Rising Stars Mathematics Half-termly Assessments* support teachers using Rising Stars Mathematics to assess whether their pupils have mastered the concepts taught in each half term. They are a tool to help teachers identify gaps in understanding and plan for future teaching, including timely interventions.

How do the tests support teachers to assess mastery?

Teachers have access to online marksheets and reports via MARK (My Assessment and Reporting Kit). These enable them to analyse the results for individual pupils and for the whole class.

The results data can be used to help teachers assess mastery. They indicate whether pupils are working at the level of 'developing mastery', 'mastery' or 'mastery with depth'. This data can then be used alongside other evidence to enable effective planning of future teaching and learning, for reporting to parents and as evidence for school-wide data collection.

About the *Rising Stars Mathematics Half-termly Assessments*

The tests cover the concepts taught in *Rising Stars Mathematics*. There is a separate test for each half term, focused on the concepts covered in that half term. For an overview of the units and concepts covered in each half term, refer to the medium-term plans in the online resources.

The content of each test is shown in the tables below:

Test	Question	Mark	NC domain	Rising Stars Mathematics unit
Autumn 1	1	1	N	1a
	2	1	N	1a
	3	1	M	1c
	4	1	M	1c
	5	1	M	1d
	6	1	A&S	2a
	7	1	M	2b
	8	2	N	1b

Test	Question	Mark	NC domain	Rising Stars Mathematics unit
Autumn 2	1	1	G	3b
	2	1	M	4b
	3	1	G	3a
	4	1	N	4a
	5	1	N	4a
	6	2	P	3c
	7	1	M	4c
	8	1	M	4c

Test	Question	Mark	NC domain	Rising Stars Mathematics unit
Spring 1	1	1	M	6a
	2	1	N	6c
	3	1	N	6b
	4	1	N	6b
	5	1	A&S	5c
	6	1	M&D	5a
	7	1	A&S	5c
	8	1	M&D, N	6c
	9	1	M	6a
	10	1	M&D	5a
	11	2	A&S	5b

Test	Question	Mark	NC domain	Rising Stars Mathematics unit
Spring 2	1	1	N	7a
	2	1	N	7b
	3	1	M	9b
	4	1	A&S	9a
	5	1	M, A&S	9b
	6	1	M	8b
	7	1	N	7b
	8	1	M	8c
	9	1	M&D	7b
	10	1	M	8a
	11	2	A&S	9a

Test	Question	Mark	NC domain	Rising Stars Mathematics unit
Summer 1	1	1	G	10b
	2	1	G	10a
	3	1	N	11a
	4	1	N	11b
	5	1	M	11c
	6	1	P	10b
	7	1	N	11b
	8	1	N	11a
	9	1	M	11c
	10	1	P	11d
	11	a) 1 b) 1	a) G b) G	10a
	12	1	A&S	11b
	13	1	G, P	10b
	14	1	N	11a

Test	Question	Mark	NC domain	Rising Stars Mathematics unit
Summer 2	1	1	F	13a
	2	1	M&D	13c
	3	1	P	14a
	4	1	A&S	12b
	5	1	A&S	12a, 12b
	6	1	A&S	12b
	7	1	A&S	12b
	8	1	F	13a
	9	1	F	13b
	10	2	F	13a, 13b
	11	1	M&D	13c
	12	1	M&D	13c
	13	1	F	14a
	14	1	P	14b

Test demand

Test demand increases both within the tests and across the year, in line with pupils' developing skills and knowledge.

Fluency, reasoning and problem solving

Each test includes a balance of fluency, reasoning and problem-solving questions. This enables teachers to assess pupils' skills and depth of knowledge in a variety of ways, as well as supporting them to fulfil the aims of the 2013 National Curriculum.

Assessing mastery

The number of marks gradually increases across the year. The marks scored in the tests can help teachers to assess whether pupils have mastered the concepts they have been taught. The marks for each test have been split into three bands:

- developing mastery
- mastery
- mastery with depth.

The table gives the mark ranges for the bands for the year group. If pupils have mastered the concepts they have been taught, they are likely to consistently score in the middle band of marks across the year. The higher the mark in the band, the more secure they are within it.

The bands should only be used as an indicator. Teachers should evaluate the results from the half-termly assessments alongside whole-class activities, the *Let's Review* tasks in the Textbook and any other activities taken through the year. A combination of formative assessment, summative assessment, daily observations and professional judgement will enable teachers to form a complete assessment of whether pupils have mastered the concepts they have been taught.

Test	Total marks	Developing mastery	Mastery	Mastery with depth
Autumn 1	9	0 to 4	5 to 8	9
Autumn 2	9	0 to 4	5 to 8	9
Spring 1	12	0 to 5	6 to 10	11 to 12
Spring 2	12	0 to 5	6 to 10	11 to 12
Summer 1	15	0 to 6	7 to 13	14 to 15
Summer 2	15	0 to 6	7 to 13	14 to 15

It is important to note that because the tests become progressively harder and longer throughout the year, teachers will not necessarily see an increase in an individual pupil's marks each time they take a test.

How to use the *Rising Stars Mathematics Half-termly Assessments*
Preparation and timings
1 Make enough copies of the test(s) for each pupil to have their own copy.
2 Hand out the papers and ensure pupils are seated appropriately so that they can't see each other's papers.
3 Pupils will need pens or pencils, rulers and erasers. However, encourage pupils to cross out answers rather than rub them out. Colouring pencils will be useful in some tests.
4 It may be useful for pupils to have access to rough paper for jottings.
5 There are no time limits for the tests but standard practice is to allow one minute per mark for written tests.

Supporting pupils during the tests
Before the test, explain to the pupils that the test is an opportunity to show what they know, understand and can do. They should try to answer all the questions but should not worry if there are some they can't do.

Many pupils will be able to work independently in the tests, with minimal support from the teacher or a teaching assistant. However, pupils should be encouraged to 'have a go' at a question, or to move on to a fresh question if they appear to be stuck, to ensure that no pupil becomes distressed.

It is important that pupils receive appropriate support, but are not unfairly advantaged or disadvantaged. Throughout the tests therefore, the teacher may read, explain or sign to a pupil any parts of the test that include instructions, for example by demonstrating how to circle an answer.

Help with reading may be given using the same rules as when providing a reader with the KS2 National Tests.

Marking the tests

Use the detailed mark scheme and professional judgement to award marks. Do not award half marks. Note that a number of questions in each test may require pupils to do more than one thing for one mark. The mark scheme provides clear guidance in the allocation of marks to support consistent marking of the tests.

It is useful to carry out peer marking of test questions from time to time. Pupils should exchange test sheets and mark them as you read out the question and answer. You will need to check that pupils are marking accurately. This approach also provides an opportunity to recap on any questions that pupils found difficult to answer.

Feeding back to pupils

Once the test has been marked, use a five-minute feedback session with the pupils to help them review their answers. Wherever possible, encourage pupils to make their own corrections. This helps them to become more aware of their own strengths and weaknesses.

A template 'My progress' sheet is provided on page x to help with this. Encourage pupils to colour the face that best shows how well they think they did in the test (there are three faces to choose from – one happy, one sad and one neutral). They should then add the number of the question they found most difficult. Finally, pupils should fill in the speech bubble to indicate what they need more help with. Some pupils will be able to do this themselves but some may find a word bank supplied by the teacher useful. The teacher or another adult may need to act as scribe for some pupils.

Using the online marksheets and reporting to analyse results

Access marksheets and reporting via MARK (My Assessment and Reporting Kit) to analyse the results for individual pupils, a class or groups of pupils.

To access the marksheets and reporting, log in to MARK (My Assessment and Reporting Kit) via the icon on your My Rising Stars dashboard (www.risingstars-uk.com/user).

If your school is accessing MARK (My Assessment and Reporting Kit) for the first time and the icon is not appearing on your dashboard, unlock your access by placing a free order at www.risingstars-uk.com/rsassessment.

Using the online tool:

- Save and print reports for individual pupils. Share these reports with them and discuss the next steps in their learning.
- Generate group reports. Group reports are ideal for monitoring specific groups of pupils, who may not be in the same class, such as those receiving pupil premium funding.

For support with using MARK (My Assessment and Reporting Kit), visit www.rsassessment.com/mark-online-support/ where there is a step-by-step guide to getting started and a useful video walkthrough, or email onlinesupport@risingstars-uk.com.

Rising Stars Mathematics Half-termly Assessments will complement your existing formative assessment, summative assessment, daily observations and professional judgement to ensure that you have an accurate picture of each pupil's level of understanding to inform future teaching and learning.

Caroline Clissold and Cherri Moseley, Series Editors

My progress

Name: _____ Class: _____ Date: _____

Test: _____

★ How well did you do?

★ Which question did you find the hardest?

★ What do you need more help with?

Year 1
Half-termly Assessment   Autumn 1

Name: _____ Class: _____ Date: _____

Note: you will need blue, yellow, green and red pencils for this test.

---

1. Write the numbers in order.

17   18   16   15

| 14 | | | | | 19 |

1 mark

---

2. Write the missing numbers.

[   ] is 1 more than 23.

[   ] is 1 less than 23.

1 mark

---

3. How many buttons long is the crayon?

CRAYON

[   ]

1 mark

---

4. Draw a taller stick person.

1 mark

/4

Total for this page

5. Circle the month that follows April.

January   May

June   July

6. Write the missing numbers.

10 − 6 = ☐

3 + ☐ = 8

7. Draw a snake four squares long using the instructions below.

- The first square is blue.
- The last square is yellow.
- The green square is next to the yellow one.
- The red square is before the green one.

/3

Total for this page

8. There are 4 rings for the abacus.

Which numbers can you make using all 4 rings?

tens   ones

2 marks

/9

Total for this test

Year 1
Half-termly Assessment Autumn 2

Name: _____ Class: _____ Date: _____

1.

How many triangles are there?

1 mark

2. What is the time on this clock?

1 mark

3. Draw lines from the shapes to their names.

cuboid   cylinder   cube

1 mark

/3

Total for this page

4. **Two** sentences are true. Tick (✓) them.

1 more than 12 is 13. ☐   1 more than 28 is 27. ☐

1 less than 25 is 26. ☐   1 less than 20 is 19. ☐

☐ 1 mark

5. Write the missing numbers in this pattern.

| 24 | ☐ | 44 | 54 | ☐ |

☐ 1 mark

6. Draw lines to match the cats to the places.

Kit   Sam   Dan

Kit is		at the side of the chair.
Sam is		under the table.
Dan is		on top of the wall.

☐ 2 marks

/4
Total for this page

7. Tick (✓) the toy that is **lighter** on each balance.

1 mark

8. Match each label to a jug of water.

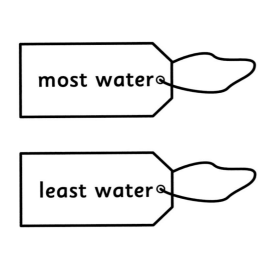

most water

least water

1 mark

/9

Total for this test

Year 1
Half-termly Assessment   Spring 1

Name: _____ Class: _____ Date: _____

1. Tick (✓) the coin that has the greatest value.

☐ 1 mark

2. Start at 0 on the number line.

Make three hops of 2 on the number line.

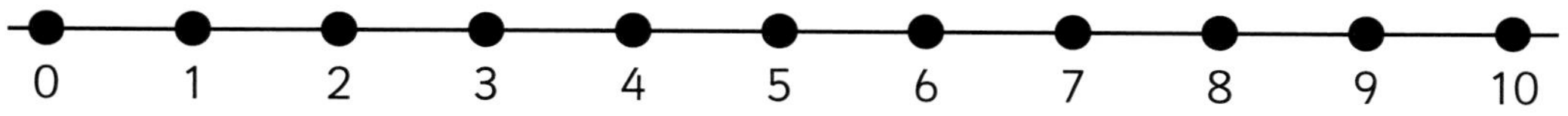

0 1 2 3 4 5 6 7 8 9 10

On what number do you finish?

☐ 1 mark

3. Write the next three numbers.

40   50   60   ____   ____   ____

☐ 1 mark

4. Write in the **two** missing numbers.

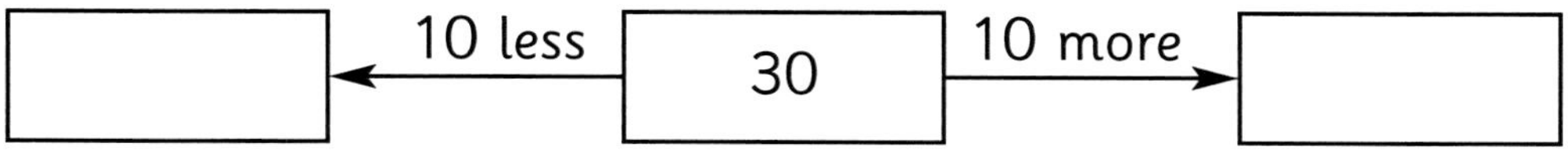

[____] ←10 less— [30] —10 more→ [____]

☐ 1 mark

/4

Total for
this page

5.   8 + 7 = ☐

6.

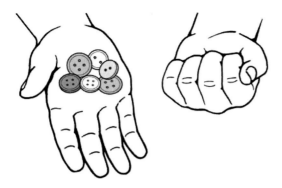

Anesh has the same number of buttons in each hand.
How many buttons has Anesh altogether?

☐ buttons

7.   There were 15 balls in the bag.

Jackie took 6 balls out of the bag.

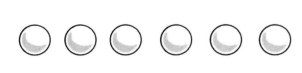

How many balls are in the bag now?

☐ balls

8.

27p   16p   19p   51p   45p

Find the even price label.

What is 2p less?

☐ P

8

9.   How much money is here?

P   ☐
                           1 mark

10. Write in the missing numbers.

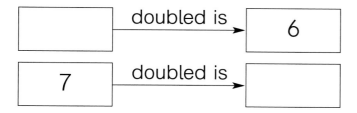

☐
1 mark

11. Write in the missing numbers.

6 + ☐ = 20   20 − 12 = ☐

4 + ☐ = 20   20 − 2 = ☐

☐
2 marks

/12

**Total for
this test**

Year 1
Half-termly Assessment   Spring 2

Name: _____   Class: _____   Date: _____

1. Draw rings to make groups of two stars.

How many groups can you make?

[   ]   [ ] 1 mark

2. How many socks are there altogether?

[   ] socks   [ ] 1 mark

3. Draw the hands on the clock to show five o'clock.

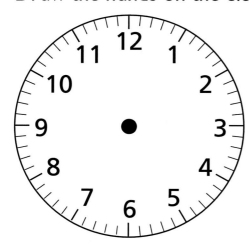

[ ] 1 mark

[ ] /3
Total for this page

4. Draw jumps on the number line to subtract 9 from 14.

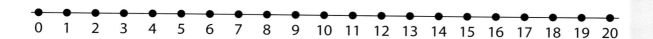

$14 - 9 =$ ☐

1 mark

5.

MONDAY	TUESDAY	WEDNESDAY	THURSDAY	FRIDAY	SATURDAY	SUNDAY
					1	2
3	4	5	6	7	8	9
10	11	12	13	14	15	16
17	18	19	20	21	22	23
24	25	26	27	28	29	30

Today is 9th. My birthday is on 17th.

How many days until my birthday?

Use the number line to find your answer.

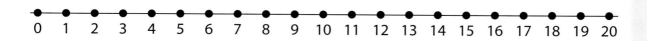

☐ days

1 mark

/2

Total for this page

6.

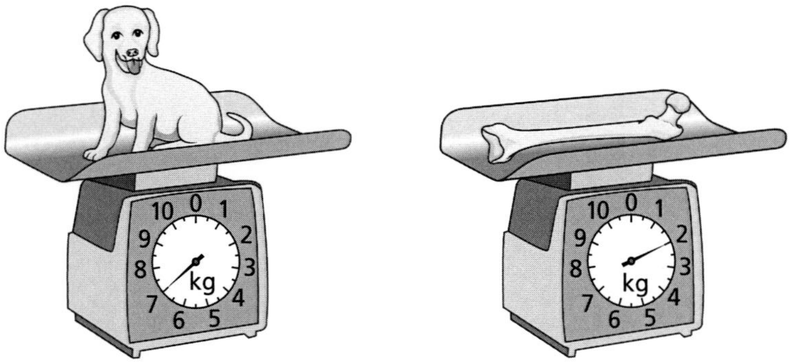

The dog eats the bone.

What is the mass of the dog now?

[ ] kg

1 mark

7.

Pete and Jen share the coins equally.

How much money will Pete get?

[ ] p

1 mark

---

8. Each jug can hold ten litres of water.

There are more litres in Jug A than Jug B.

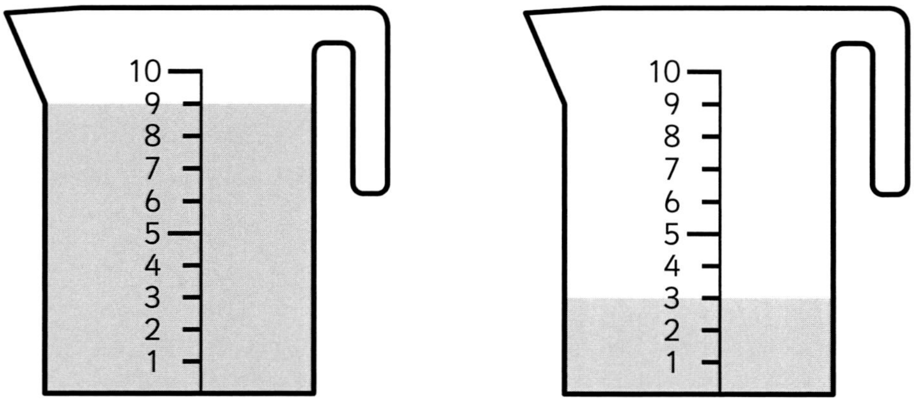

Jug A **Jug B**

How many more?

[ ] litres

1 mark

/3

Total for this page

© Rising Stars UK Ltd 2017. You may photocopy this page.

9. Harry shares these cakes equally between three plates.

How many cakes are on each plate?

	cakes

10. Tick (✓) the line that is 8 cm long.

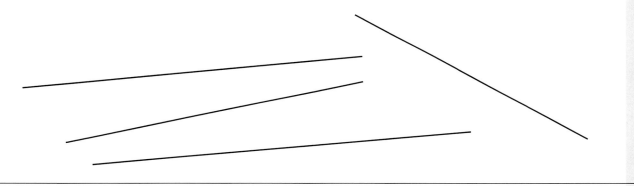

11. Write an addition and a subtraction statement for this number line.

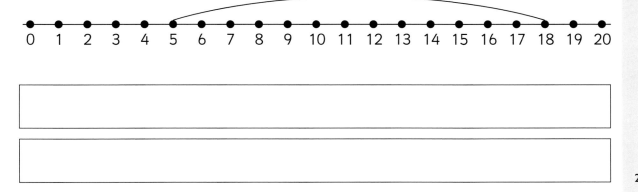

/12

**Total for
this test**

Year 1
Half-termly Assessment   Summer 1

Name: _____   Class: _____   Date: _____

1.  ○ △ □ □ ○ △ □ ○ ○ △ □ □

Tick (✓) the mistake in the pattern.

1 mark

2. Match each drawing of a 3-D shape to its name.

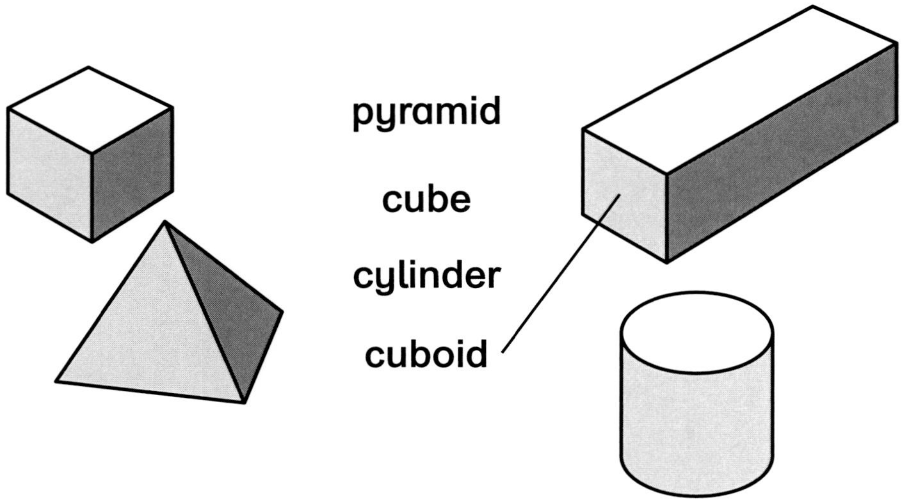

pyramid

cube

cylinder

cuboid

1 mark

3. Tick (✓) the child who is third in the race.

1 mark

/3

Total for this page

4. **Two** sentences are true. Tick (✓) them.

5 more than 35 is 40. ☐   5 more than 25 is 35. ☐

5 less than 30 is 20. ☐   5 less than 20 is 15. ☐

1 mark

---

5. Tick (✓) the clock that shows half past eight.

1 mark

---

6. Put your finger on the **Start** square.

- Turn right
- Forward 2
- Turn left
- Forward 3.

Draw a cross (✗) in the square you stop at.

Start			

☐

1 mark

/3

Total for
this page

7. Write the missing numbers in this pattern.

| 25 | | 35 | 40 | |

8. Write the numbers in order on the line, starting with the **smallest**.

47   27   31   74

9. Draw the hands on the clock to show the time half an hour earlier.

10.

Tick (✓) the next marble in the pattern.

16

11.

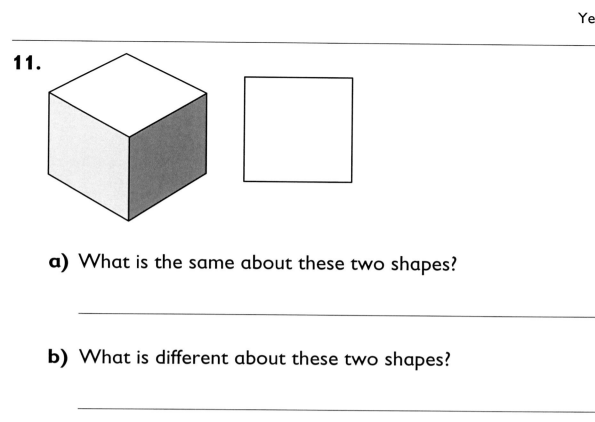

   a) What is the same about these two shapes?

_____

1 mark

   b) What is different about these two shapes?

_____

1 mark

12. There are 25 balls in the bag.

Jackie puts 5 more balls in the bag.

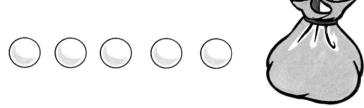

How many are in the bag now?

| balls |

1 mark

/3

Total for
this page

13.

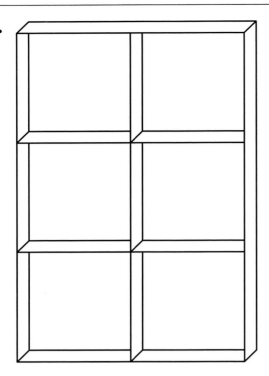

Draw a circle on the right hand side of the top shelf.

Draw a triangle on the left hand side of the middle shelf.

Draw a rectangle on the shelf above the triangle.

1 mark

14. Here are three digit cards.

1   **3**   **7**

Use the cards to make 2-digit numbers.

Write the numbers in the correct order.

1 **3** , ☐☐ , ☐☐ , ☐☐ , ☐☐ , ☐☐

smallest   **largest**

1 mark

/15

Total for this test

Name: _____   Class: _____   Date: _____

1.

Circle **half** of these coins.

How much money is half?

£ [   ]

1 mark

2.

```
0  1  2  3  4  5  6  7  8  9  10  11  12  13  14  15  16  17  18  19  20
```

How many fives make 15?

[   ]

1 mark

3. Look at the girl's face in the first box.

The girl makes a half turn.

Tick (✓) the picture that shows her after she makes the half turn.

1 mark

/3

Total for this page

19

4.

17	
9	8

Write a subtraction calculation to match the bar model.

_____

1 mark

5. Add 3 more grapes.

Complete the bars to show many grapes there are now.

	3

1 mark

6. 11 birds are on the branch.

4 birds fly away.

How many are left? ☐ birds

Write a number sentence that shows how to work it out.

1 mark

/3

Total for
this page

20

7. Adam has 9 white cubes and 5 blue cubes.

How many more white cubes than blue cubes does he have?

| cubes |

1 mark

8. Ben has 12 counters.

He has half of the counters in each hand.

How many counters has he in each hand?

| counters |

1 mark

9. Circle one quarter of these stars.

☆ ☆ ☆ ☆

☆ ☆ ☆ ☆

☆ ☆ ☆ ☆

1 mark

/3

Total for
this page

10. Write $\frac{1}{4}$ or $\frac{1}{2}$ to show the fraction shaded.

☐/☐ ☐/☐ ☐/☐ ☐/☐

2 marks

11. Harry, Jax, Kate and Danuta share these sweets.

They get the same number each.

How many sweets do they each get?

☐ sweets

1 mark

12. Tom puts flowers into bunches of 5.

There are 4 bunches.

How many flowers are there?

☐ flowers

1 mark

/4

Total for this page

13. Colour part of the large square so that $\frac{1}{4}$ of the large square is white.

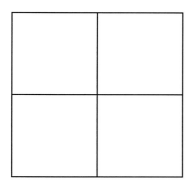

1 mark

14. Complete the table to show the directions the turtle moves to reach the square.

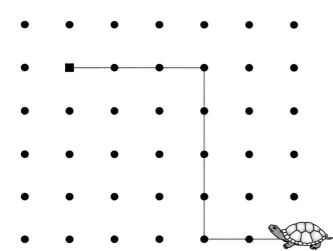

| Forward 2 |
| ¼ turn right |
| |
| |
| Forward 3 |

1 mark

/15

Total for this test

Answers and mark schemes

Year 1 Autumn

Test 1		Mark	NC domain	Rising Stars Mathematics unit	Additional information
1.	15, 16, 17, 18	1	N	1a	Award 1 mark for all correct.
2.	24 and 22	1	N	1a	Award 1 mark for both correct.
3.	6	1	M	1c	
4.	Draws taller stick person	1	M	1c	
5.	Circles May	1	M	1d	Accept any other clear way of indicating the correct month.
6.	4, 5	1	A&S	2a	Award 1 mark for both correct.
7.	Draws squares in this order: blue, red, green, yellow	1	M	2b	Squares do not need to be drawn accurately. Squares do not need to be in a straight line but should be connected and in the correct order.
8.	40, 31, 22, 13, 4	2	N	1b	Award 2 marks for finding all numbers. Award 1 mark for finding three numbers.
Total marks: 9					

Year 1 Autumn

Test 2		Mark	NC domain	Rising Stars Mathematics unit	Additional information
1.	3	1	G	3b	
2.	7 o'clock	1	M	4b	Accept 7, 7:00 a.m. or 7:00 or similar.
3.	cuboid cylinder cube	1	G	3a	Award 1 mark for all correct.
4.	Ticks 1 more than 12 is **13** and 1 less than 20 is **19**.	1	N	4a	Award 1 mark for both correct and no others.
5.	34, 64	1	N	4a	Award 1 mark for both correct.
6.	Kit is — at the side of the chair. / Sam is — under the table. / Dan is — on top of the wall.	2	P	3c	Award 2 marks for all three correct. Award 1 mark for two correct.
7.	Ticks dragon on the left-hand scale **and** ticks ball on the right-hand scale	1	M	4c	Accept any other clear way of indicating the correct toys. Award 1 mark for both correct.
8.	most water least water	1	M	4c	Accept any clear labelling.
Total marks: 9					

Year 1 Spring

Test 1		Mark	NC domain	Rising Stars Mathematics unit	Additional information
1.	Ticks the £1 coin	1	M	6a	Accept correct answer with no markings on the number line.
2.	6	1	N	6c	Award 1 mark for evidence of three hops of 2 or a correct answer of 6.
3.	70, 80, 90	1	N	6b	Award 1 mark for all three correct.
4.	20 and 40	1	N	6b	Award 1 mark for both correct.
5.	15	1	A&S	5c	
6.	12	1	M&D	5a	
7.	9	1	A&S	5c	
8.	14	1	N	6c	
9.	20	1	M	6a	
10.	3, 14	1	M&D	5a	Award 1 mark for both correct.
11.	14, 8 16, 18	2	A&S	5b	Award 1 mark for each two correct.
Total marks: 12					

Year 1 Spring

Test 2	Mark	NC domain	Rising Stars Mathematics unit	Additional information
1. Circles 6 groups of 2 stars 6	1	N	7a	Award 1 mark for pairs of stars circled as well as correct answer 6.
2. 16	1	N	7b	
3. Hands showing 5 o'clock	1	M	9b	Ignore length of hands.
4. 5	1	A&S	9a	Award 1 mark for jumps on number line as well as correct answer 7.
5. 8	1	M, A&S	9b	Award 1 mark for number line showing 8 jumps from 9 to 17, or other jump(s) from 9 to 17, as well as correct answer 8.
6. 9	1	M	8b	
7. 50	1	N	7b	
8. 6	1	M	8c	
9. 5	1	M&D	7b	
10.	1	M	8a	
11. 5 + 13 = 18, 18 − 13 = 5	2	A&S	9a	Award 1 mark for each correct.
Total marks: 12				

Year 1 Summer

Test 1		Mark	NC domain	Rising Stars Mathematics unit	Additional information
1.	Ticks 8th shape	1	G	10b	Accept any other clear way of indicating the incorrect shape.
2.		1	G	10a	Award 1 mark for all correct.
3.	Ticks 3rd runner	1	N	11a	Accept any other clear way of indicating the third runner.
4.	Ticks 5 more than 35 is 40 **and** 5 less than 20 is 15.	1	N	11b	Award 1 mark for both correct and no others.
5.	Ticks 4th clock	1	M	11c	Accept any other clear way of indicating the fourth clock.
6.		1	P	10b	Allow any mark in the correct square.
7.	30, 45	1	N	11b	Award 1 mark for both correct.
8.	27, 31, 47, 74	1	N	11a	
9.		1	M	11c	Ignore length of hands.
10.		1	P	11d	Accept any other clear way of indicating the third marble.

Test 1	Mark	NC domain	Rising Stars Mathematics unit	Additional information
11. a) Both are made from square/ squares	**a)** 1	**a)** G	10a	Accept similar explanations.
b) Square is a 2D shape/is one square, cube is 3D/has 6 square faces	**b)** 1	**b)** G		
12. 30	1	A&S	11b	
13.	1	G, P	10b	Award 1 mark for all three correct.
14. 17, 31, 37, 71, 73	1	N	11a	Award 1 mark for all five correct.
Total marks: 15				

Year 1 Summer

Test 2	Mark	NC domain	Rising Stars Mathematics unit	Additional information
1. Circles 5 coins £5	1	F	13a	Award 1 mark for both 5 coins circled and £5.
2. 3	1	M&D	13c	
3. Circles girl facing backwards	1	P	14a	
4. Any of these subtractions: $17 - 9 = 8$, $8 = 17 - 9$, $17 - 8 = 9$, $9 = 17 - 8$	1	A&S	12b	
5. 11 top bar 8 bottom bar	1	A&S	12a, 12b	Award mark for 11 in top bar only.
6. 7 $11 - 4 = 7$	1	A&S	12b	Award 1 mark for both correct.
7. 4	1	A&S	12b	
8. 6	1	F	13a	
9. Circles 3 stars	1	F	13b	
10. $\frac{1}{2}$, $\frac{1}{2}$, $\frac{1}{4}$, $\frac{1}{2}$	2	F	13a, 13b	Accept $\frac{2}{4}$ for $\frac{1}{2}$ Award 2 marks for all four correct. Award 1 mark for any three correct.
11. 3	1	M&D	13c	
12. 20	1	M&D	13c	
13. Any quarter white so any 3 squares to be shaded	1	F	14a	
14. Forward 4 $\frac{1}{4}$ turn left	1	P	14b	Award 1 mark for both correct. Accept any spelling errors as long as intention is clear. Accept 'F' for 'forward' and 'L' for left. Do not accept $\frac{4}{1}$ for $\frac{1}{4}$
Total marks: 15				